Marriage Wisdom Moments

31 Days to a Better Marriage

Loretta A. Pittman

Library of Congress 2020917200
ISBN-13: 978-0-578-72462-1

DEDICATION

I dedicate this book to my Lord and Savior Jesus Christ for the wisdom he has allowed me to have to write this book, because without God it is impossible, but with God all things are possible. I also dedicate this book to my handsome and wonderful husband William K. Pittman whom God has allowed to walk with me on this journey called life. I love you honey, and I am so honored to be called your wife. I also want to dedicate this book to my grown children, grandchildren and future grandchildren and great grandchildren I love you all so much.

ACKNOWLEDGMENTS

I Give all glory and praise and honor to My Lord and savior who chose me for this assignment. He has taught me the true meaning of a covenant relationship. We as married couples need to understand that the covenant relationship, we have with God is a reflection of the covenant relationship we have with our spouses. If we are cheating on our spouses, then we are cheating on God. If we are lying and sneaking around on our spouses were also lying and sneaking around on God. Do you see how that works?

1st Peter 3:7 says, In the same way, you husbands must give honor to your wives. Treat your wife with understanding as you live together. She may be weaker than you are, but she is your equal partner in God's gift of new life. Treat her as you should so your prayers will not be hindered. When you treat your spouse with love and respect you will be treated the same way and God will Bless you because of it. The marriage covenant is so important to God.

Introduction

Moments in our lives should be so important, every day we have different moments with each other whether it is an intimate moment, a family moment or pregnancy moment whatever the moment it is all important. Sometimes we get so busy in our lives that we miss crucial moments in each other lives, like when the baby starts walking or talking. When we do miss that moment, we think about how we should have been more present and in that moment. Well this is what Marriage Wisdom Moments is about, being present in the current state of your marriage whether good or bad.

If your marriage is good, then this book will enhance what you already have and make you more aware of present moments you share with your spouse. If your marriage is bad, then this book will help you to get on the right road to having better and more loving marriage moments with your spouse. Marriage is a journey just like life and the person you decide to take with you on that journey should be trust worthy, loving ,kind and willing to learn and they should want the same things in life like you do. If you are on a journey with someone who is always going against you then how can you be successful? The bible says in **Amos 3:3 (NLT) Can two people walk together without agreeing on the direction?** God designed marriage to be a covenant relationship like the one we should have with him, meaning we are married to God once we decide to walk in the life that he predestinated for us. God designed marriage the same way for us to walk together as one in that predestinated life he set before us. We are to walk it through until the end no matter what circumstances come up along the way. **Romans 8:30 says, and those whom he predestined he also called, and those whom he called he also justified, and those whom he justified he also glorified.**

Having a daily relationship with God is so important and it is a reflection of the relationship you have with your spouse. If your relationship with your spouse is good, then your relationship with God is good. **1 Peter 3:7 says, "You husbands in the same way, live with your wives in an**

understanding way, as with someone weaker, since she is a woman; and show her honor as a fellow heir of the grace of life, so that your prayers will not be hindered. Now you can see if your relationship is not good with your spouse your prayers will be hindered and that means your relationship will not be good with God. When your relationship gets bad that means it is time for you to start building a relationship with Christ, we need God to help us through the moments that we encounter in our marriages.

The first thing you should know, and this is where a lot of marriages get in trouble and that is putting your spouse before God and making them your everything or professing that they are your everything. This is a form of Idolatry and God does not like it. **Exodus 20:1-17 says, And God spake all these words, saying, I am the Lord thy God, which have brought thee out of the land of Egypt, out of the house of bondage. Thou shalt have no other gods before me. Thou**

shalt not make unto thee any graven image, or any likeness of any thing that is in heaven above, or that is in the earth beneath, or that is in the water under the earth. Thou shalt not bow down thyself to them, nor serve them: for I the Lord thy God am a jealous God, visiting the iniquity of the fathers upon the children unto the third and fourth generation of them that hate me; And shewing mercy unto thousands of them that love me, and keep my commandments. As you can see it is also a sin to make your spouse your everything.

God needs to be first because he created you and your spouse so, to put them before God in your life becomes sin. That was one of the things my husband and I had to over come in our marriage and once we realized what the word of God said about that we asked God to change our hearts so that we loved each other but that we both would love him first together. **Ecclesiastes 4:12 says, two people can resist an attack that would defeat one person alone. A rope made of three cords**

is hard to break. This scripture lets you know that God is that common denominator in any marriage If you do not have God meaning **(Father, Son and Holy Spirit)** you do not have a marriage. When a husband and a wife make God their everything together, they will always win no matter what! because God honors himself being first in their lives. Can you see how God feels about being first? It is the same as a wife or husband desiring to be first in their spouse's life. Think about it you married your spouse, but you decide to treat your friends' spouse better than you treat yours is that right or is that wrong?

It is totally wrong! if you married your spouse, they should be treated better than anyone else but not worshipped. **1Kings 14:9 says, you have done more evil than all who came before you. You have proceeded to make for yourself other gods and molten images to provoke Me, and you have flung Me behind your back. (BSB version).** When we decide to remove God from our marriage, we have removed all coverings and blessings he has instore for you. Separation and divorce do not just happen! you lost communication with God as the head of your marriage and you lost communication with your spouse. Marriage Wisdom Moments will help jump start you on the road or back on the road to a better and more loving relationship with God as well as with your spouse. Prayer is the key communication for God and for your spouse. When you use prayer to communicate with God, he will answer whatever you pray for your spouse.

Prayer is the way that works but when you pray it cannot be selfish. You see that's where you also get in trouble with God praying selfish prayers like God make my spouse love me more or God change my spouse from their bad attitude towards me, No the key to answered prayer is to pray what God says about your spouse like **Dear heavenly Father I thank you for (put Spouses name) and I thank you for loving (Spouses name)as well as loving me. Thank you, Lord, that your word says a threefold cord**

is not easily broken and I know by your word that we are both spiritually and wonderfully made. Please help my spouse and I overcome this (whatever the problem is) because your word says we can do all things through Christ that strengthens us. Do you see how you placed your spouse and you in God's hands? by including him as the head of your prayer and not making it just about what you want. Real prayer and **Answered** prayer are humbling yourself and your issue in the presence of God but also speaking boldly using his word. Remember you have the **Victory** no matter where you are in your marriage. **Prayer changes things.**

Take this simple quiz to see how satisfied you are in your marriage.

Test Your Own Marriage Satisfaction

Marital relationships are complex institutions! To improve the quality of a marriage, it helps to take a systematic look at how it is functioning. Here is a questionnaire you can use as a general guide for evaluating your marital satisfaction.

After each question below write down the number that most closely approximates your present feelings about your marriage or your spouse. On a scale of one to ten, 10 is "pleased," 5 is "half yes/half no," and 0 is "not pleased."

I am:

Pleased with the amount we talk to each other.

Happy with the friends we share in common.

Satisfied with our sex life.

In agreement with the amount of time you or we spend at work and at home.

In agreement with the way we are spending money.

Pleased with the kind of parent you are. (This refers to the way your spouse interacts with the children.)

Of the opinion that you are "on my team."

Pleased with our leisure time together (e.g., sports, vacations, outings, etc.).

Basically, in agreement with your outlook on life (e.g., values, attitudes, religious beliefs, politics, etc.).

Generally pleased with the way you relate to members of your own family. (This refers to your spouse's parents, siblings, etc.)

Satisfied with the way you relate to members of my family. (This refers to your own parents, siblings, etc.)

Pleased with your general habits, mannerisms, and overall appearance.

Add up your total score:

84 and more means that you have a VERY GOOD marriage.

Between 72-83 reflects SATISFACTORY to GOOD feelings and interactions.

A score of 61-71 suggests that you need to make some basic changes.

Below 60 indicates a POOR level of marital satisfaction. The information in this book is going to help you practice better loving moments in your marriage and help you be more present for all situations you encounter in your marriage. Daily Marriage Wisdom is the key to solving all your marital issues.

COMMUNICATION

Marriage Wisdom Moments

Day 1

Amos 3:3 Says: Can Two Walk together unless they have agreed to do so.

Inspiration: What can the married couple do to ensure that their marriage will last? The first and most important issue is learning how to live on one accord. If both of you are always on opposite ends of every issue you will never live in harmony. Start agreeing on the small things and work your way up to the bigger things until you are totally in agreement on all things. **Be Blessed!**

Practice: Take this day to begin to agree on the important issues in your marriage and then everyday start to choose to agree on more and more issues and then one day you will see your marriage coming closer and closer together.

Prayer: Dear heavenly Father please help me, and my spouse become one by allowing us opportunities to agree with each other as you lead us. Your word says in **Matthew 18:19 "Again I say to you, that if two of you agree on earth about anything that they may ask, it shall be done for them by My Father who is in heaven.** We understand you made marriage so help us live out your plan for us to be on one accord in our marriage. Thank you, Lord, for all your help in this matter in **Jesus Name Amen!**

LOVE

Marriage Wisdom Moments

Day 2

Romans 15:7 Says: Accept one another then just as Christ accepted you to bring praise to God.

Inspiration: The key to a long-lasting marriage is to stop trying to change the other person. Love that person for who they are and accept them the way they are. If you absolutely loved them, you would not try to change them. **Be Blessed!**

Practice: Take today to look at the reality of your spouse and see what you really have in that person. Then decide that no matter how they behave and what they look like you will love them and not try to change them. Love them where they are and accept what you see, and you will have a happier marriage.

Prayer: Dear heavenly father help me accept the things that I can't change in my spouse and help me to see them through your eyes and to love them the way they are and not the way I want them to be. **Romans 15:5-7 says, Now may the God who gives perseverance and encouragement grant you to be of the same mind with one another according to Christ Jesus, so that with one accord you may with one voice glorify the God and Father of our Lord Jesus Christ. Therefore, accept one another, just as Christ also accepted us to the glory of God**.

Let me love my spouse the way you would have me to love him/her and leave any changes that I desire to be made to you. Your word also says **in Psalm 37:4 Delight yourself in the Lord, and he will give you the desires of your heart.** I thank you that my marriage and covenant before you are moving into the right direction and I thank you for giving me the desires of my heart in **Jesus Name Amen!**

TRUST

Marriage Wisdom Moments

Day 3

Psalm 20:4 Says: May he give you the desires of your heart and make all your plans succeed.

Inspiration: Man and woman of God stop looking to your spouse for all your happiness. God did not design man or woman to handle that much power. God is the only one who can handle that much power and therefore is the only one we should be putting all our happiness and trust in. When you leave all your happiness in the hands of your spouse, they will disappoint you every time because God says, there shall be no one above him that means not even your spouse. **Be Blessed!**

God is the only one who knows truly how to make us happy so trust God over your spouse to make you happy. Tell God what you desire in your spouse and watch him change your spouse in ways you never though he could. Only God can live through us to give each spouse their hearts desire.

Practice: Take today and begin to tell God what you desire in your spouse and make sure to give God details of what you desire and watch God do everything you have asked and more. Be ready for God to change you first so you can handle your new and changed spouse.

Prayer: Dear heavenly Father thank you so much for giving me my heart's desire through **(Spouses Name)**. I now know I have been putting all my trust and happiness in the wrong place and that all the glory and honor belongs to you. **Exodus 20:3 says "You shall have no other gods before me.** Thank you for opening my eyes to this matter and I now know that putting my spouse before you is not what you desire me to do. Thank you that this prayer is done! In **Jesus Name Amen!**

RESPECT

Marriage Wisdom Moments

Day 4

Ephesians 5:33 Says: So again, I say each man must love his wife as he loves himself and the wife must respect her husband.

Inspiration: You cannot keep putting your spouse down and then expect them to love and respect you later, it just does not work that way. How about complementing them on what they are doing right instead of what they are doing wrong. Love your spouse where they are and pray for the things you believe they could do better. **Philippians 4:13 says we can do all things through Christ who strengthens us,** so stop speaking negative words and start speaking words of encouragement and watch your spouse grow, love, and respect you like never. **Be Blessed!**

Practice: Take this week to speak to your spouse with respect. If you are a person who curse to communicate, or yell then ask God to help you to stop and help you to speak with respect and just see how your spouse responds. Also speak encouraging words over your spouse and watch them grow.

Prayer: Dear Heavenly Father I (Put your name) come to you surrendering my will for your will this week concerning my disrespectful ways of communicating with (Spouses Name). **Proverbs 12:25 (ESV) says, "Anxiety in a man's heart weighs him down, but a good word makes him glad."** Help me Lord to speak with respect to my spouse and help me to speak life over my spouse and speak life more abundantly. I do love my spouse and I do desire for my marriage to last and be happy.

 Help me to respect my spouse and in return they will show me love and respect also. **Galatians 6:7 says, Do not be deceived: God cannot be mocked. A man reaps what he sows,** and I thank you that it is done! **In Jesus Name Amen.!**

DISAGREEMENTS

Marriage Wisdom Moments

Day 5

Proverbs 16:25 Says: There is a way that seems right to a man, but in the end, it leads to death.

Inspiration: Be careful of right fighting, right fighting is arguing to such a degree that you would much rather prove you are right than to save the marriage. Sometimes you are being so adamant about proving to your spouse that your way is the right way that it can cause a death in your relationship. Let us be careful because God is the only one who is right. **Be Blessed!**

Practice: Today let us focus on what is most important and stop always thinking you are right, or your way is always right. Pray for God to teach you his right way and let him direct your conversation.

Prayer: Dear Heavenly Father help me (Insert your name) not to think that I am always right, and my spouse is always wrong. Help me to see that it is just a form of pride and that **Proverbs 16:18 (NIRV) says, if you are proud, you will be destroyed. If you are proud, you will fall**. Father I do not want to fall, and I do not want my marriage to die because of my prideful ways.

Romans 3:4 says, "God forbid: yea, let God be true, but every man a liar; Help me get delivered of this spirit and keep and have a spirit of being grateful and humble. I love you Lord and I love my spouse and I just desire to be the best Husband/Wife as possible in your sight. I Thank you Lord that this prayer is answered in **Jesus Name Amen!**

SEX

Marriage Wisdom Moments

Day 6

1 Corinthians 7:5 Says: Do Not deprive one another, except perhaps by agreement for a limited time that you may devote yourselves to prayer, but then come together again, so that Satan may not tempt you because of your lack of self-control.

Inspiration: Do not hold out sexually on your husband or wife even if your mad. The word of God clearly states that the devil will tempt you for your inconsistency with one another. Sex is an especially important part of the marriage life and we should be enjoying it the way God intended. Do not let the devil cause you to be inconsistent. **Be Blessed!**

Practice: If you have been using sex as a weapon against your spouse then take this week to stop it Now. Your spouse need sex because that very act also expresses their love for you. Start enjoying sex and have fun. Let God bless you both in the bedroom.

Prayer: Dear Heavenly Father forgive me for using sex as a weapon against my spouse. **1 Corinthians 7:2-5) says, but since there is so much immorality, each man should have his own wife, and each woman her own husband. The husband should fulfill his marital duty to his wife, and likewise the wife to her husband. The wife's body does not belong to her alone but also to her husband. In the same way, the husband's body does not belong to him alone but also to his wife.**

Help me not to withhold sex anymore from my spouse and let sexual healing take place in me now! Help me to be ready and available to my spouse even when I am angry or not in the mood. I now understand that sex is one of the ways my spouse shows me love, deliver me right now in **Jesus Name Amen!**

FINANCES

Marriage Wisdom Moments

Day 7

1 Timothy 6:17 Says: As for the rich in this world charge them not to be proud and arrogant and contemptuous of others, nor set their hopes on uncertain riches, but on God who richly and seamlessly provide us with everything for our enjoyment.

Inspiration: Do not set all your hopes and dreams on your finances, remember it is God who gives you power to get wealth to be a blessing to the kingdom. Put all your hopes into Gods hands. He is the only one who can make your hopes and dreams come true. Money will dwindle but God is a sure thing. You should not be basing your marriage on finances to the point that you start talking about divorce or suicide money is just that money! and if you ask God he can help you get more. **Be Blessed!**

Practice: Do not focus on money this week or your lack of money. Tell God what your hopes and dreams are and ask him to show you how to make them come to pass. Remember prayer changes any situation and that means money. God is the one who owns it all.

Prayer: Dear Heavenly Father help me make my hopes and dreams come to pass by your spirit **Malachi 3:10 says, Bring the whole tithe into the storehouse, that there may be food in my house. Test me in this," says the LORD Almighty, "and see if I will not throw open the floodgates of heaven and pour out so much blessing that there will not be room enough to store it**.

Your word also states in **Luke 6:38 Give, and it will be given to you. A good measure, pressed down, shaken together, and running over, will be poured into your lap. For with the measure you use, it will be measured to you."** Help my spouse and I obey your word to become cheerful givers so we can partake in the financial blessings you have mentioned in your word. Thank you that this prayer is answered in **Jesus Name Amen!**

DATE NIGHT

Marriage Wisdom Moments

Let us do dinner together. Let us take tonight to make dinner together. Let us decide what to make and then plan to make it. Let us find a sitter for the kids if you have some. Then cook and set the table in a romantic atmosphere, setting the tone for some sexy conversation that will lead to some powerful love making to top off the evening.

Date night simplified:

1. Let us cook together and decide what to make.
2. Let us find a sitter if need be.
3. Let us set the atmosphere for some romance.
4. Let us have a sexy conversation.
5. Top off the night with some powerful love making.

Communication

Marriage Wisdom Moments

Day 8

Mathew 12:37 Says: But I tell you that men will have to give an account on the day of judgment for every careless word they have spoken, for by your words you will be acquitted and by your words you will be condemned.

Inspiration: How we communicate towards one another is especially important to God. We should not be spewing hateful words towards one another. Some time you can think you are saying something soft or in love, but if you really listen to your tone you are really speaking harsh. Let us listen to how we are communicating. Do you yell at your spouse across the room? Are you whining and complaining about everything? Are you using profanity just to make your point? Then change it today! **Talking, Tone and Timing**

not yelling, and cursing is the key. **Be Blessed!**

Practice: Take the time to listen to how your communicating with your spouse and write down what you hear and see in yourself. Are you acting like a child or are you acting like your parents? If so, take this week to examine you and start communicating on a more positive level. Speak in a nicer tone and speak with love. Remember to listen to your tone, listen to how your talking and pay attention to your timing. **Talking, Tone and Timing.**

Prayer: Dear Heavenly Father help me to be a better communicator towards my spouse. Help me speak in love and with a nicer tone. **Ephesians 4:29 says, let no corrupting talk come out of your mouths, but only such as is good for building up, as fits the occasion, that it may give grace to those who hear.** Help me to hear and to realize when I have spoken to my spouse in a nasty and harsh tone and help me to correct it quickly and not let the enemy use me against my spouse with my mouth. Let me speak blessing over my spouse and not ill will. Help me to recognize the Tone I'm using to speak to my spouse as wells as how I am talking to him whether I'm yelling or cursing or not, help me also to know the right timing to speak to my spouse about whatever the situation may be at the right moment. Thank you, that my prayer is answered in, **Jesus Name Amen!**

LOVE

Marriage Wisdom Moments

DAY 9

Ephesians 5:25 Says: Husbands love your wives even as Christ also loved the church and gave himself for it.

Inspiration: Husbands do not say you love your wife when you are talking to her like a child. A true and loving husband will lead by the example of Christ who loves the church. Jesus died for the church, so husbands need to love their wives with everything they have. If you want your wife to respect you then love your wife like the bible says. Show her by your actions not just by your words. **Be Blessed!**

Practice: Husbands start treating your wife as an equal partner in your marriage and show her you love her. Take this week to help with the kids, clean the house, or cook dinner for her. Give her a massage or plan for her favorite flowers and candy to arrive for her. Just show her you love her like Christ love the church. You cannot expect her to respect you if you are not giving her love.

Prayer: Dear Heavenly Father, teach me how to love my wife like Christ love the church. Teach me what she likes and how she likes to be loved so I am not loving her in my own way. **Ephesians 5:28 says, In this same way, husband's ought to love their wives as their own bodies. He who loves his wife loves himself.** As you teach me Lord your way in loving her like the church and like I love myself. I will obey what you want In **Jesus Name Amen!**

TRUST

Marriage Wisdom Moments

DAY 10

Proverbs 3:30 Says: Do not accuse anyone for no reason when they have done no harm to you.

Inspiration: Let us not treat our spouse like they are constantly on trial for something they may have done in the past that caused a mistrust in your marriage. After you have forgiven them for the wrong, they may have done. Stop acting like the judge and the jury and keep convicting them of that same crime., even the court of law only sentence you once. **Be Blessed!**

Practice: Take the time this week to let go of whatever that situation is or was that has caused a mistrust in your marriage and let

God heal your marriage now! Sometimes when your holding on to that old situation it can cause your marriage not to move on to the blessings God have for your marriage. Learn how to let go and let God. He knows each one of your faults and do not hold it against you once you repent and turn from your wicked ways.

Prayer: Dear Heavenly Father, please help me to let go of the past and the thing that has caused a mistrust in my marriage. **Luke 6:37 says, do not judge, and you will not be judged. Do not condemn, and you will not be condemned. Forgive, and you will be forgiven.** Help me to truly forgive my spouse for the mistrust and help me to trust him/her again.

Matthew 18:21-22 says, then Peter came to Jesus and asked, "Lord, how many times shall I forgive my brother or sister who

sins against me? Up to seven times?" Jesus answered, "I tell you, not seven times, but seventy-seven times."

I love you lord and thank you for helping me to truly forgive. Lord I will no longer keep this situation over my spouse's head and therefore keeping myself and our marriage hostage. I thank you now for my deliverance in **Jesus Name Amen!**

RESPECT

Marriage Wisdom Moments

DAY 11

Ephesians 5:22 Says: Wives submit yourselves unto your own husbands as unto the Lord.

Inspiration: Wives sometimes do not want to submit to our own husbands because we think they will walk all over us but let us respect them enough to do what they ask within reason. Trust God over him and his attitude, God will judge his actions. If it is something you are not comfortable with then pray that God will lead you both. **Be Blessed!**

Practice: Take the time today to do something the way your spouse asked you to do it and do not complain. If he asks you to run an errand trust him enough to follow it through, again if it is something, you are not comfortable with doing take it to God in prayer.

Prayer: Dear Heavenly Father help me to do what my husband ask with respect as longs as it is right in your sight. **Ephesians 5:24 says, but as the church is subject to Christ, so also the wives ought to be to their husbands in everything.** Your word also states in **1 Peter 5:6 Therefore humble yourselves under the mighty hand of God, that He may exalt you at the proper time,** Thank you for helping me do what your words says which is respect my husband In **Jesus Name Amen!**

DISAGREEMENTS

Marriage Wisdom Moments

DAY 12

Proverbs 17:14 Says: The beginning of strife is as when water first trickles from a cracked dam; therefore, stop confrontation before it becomes worse and quarreling breaks out!

Inspiration: Stop a stupid argument before it becomes a big fight, sometimes were talking about something stupid and before you know it were arguing and saying things you do not mean. Learn how to stop right in the middle of that conversation and change the topic to something more pleasant. **Be Blessed!**

Practice: Take this day to only discuss the important things in your marriage and beware of the tone you are using when you are having the discussion. Make sure you avoid topics that you know will start a stupid argument with your spouse. Keep your conversation loving and laughable.

Prayer: Dear Heavenly Father help me not to start stupid arguments with my spouse. Help me to keep away from topics that I know will start a stupid argument. **2 Timothy 2:23-24 says, do not have anything to do with foolish and stupid arguments, because you know they produce quarrels. And the LORD's servant must not be quarrelsome but must be kind to everyone, able to teach, not resentful.** Help me to talk only about things that will edify my spouse and our marriage. Thank you for keeping us together and making us one **In Jesus Name Amen!**

SEX

Marriage Wisdom Moments

DAY 13

Song of Solomon 1-2 Says: Let him kiss me with the kisses of his mouth for thy love is better than wine.

Inspiration: Let us start enjoying sex. God made it for us to express our love and to have Godly offspring. God intended for us to be intoxicated with the love of our spouse. If we are making good love to one another, we will not have lust for other people. Let us enjoy sex the way God would have it to be. **Be Blessed!**

Practice: Let us take tonight to have more fun in the bedroom. Let us try something new or let us just enjoy whatever our heart desires. Let us invite God into our bedrooms and ask the holy ghost to teach you how to please your spouse remember God designed sex so he would know. God knows our hearts and desires.

Prayer: Dear Heavenly Father we invite you into our bedroom to teach us how to please one another and to teach us how to really have fun. **Song of Solomon 1:2-4 says, let him kiss me with the kisses of his mouth: for thy love [is] better than wine.** It also says in **Proverbs 5:19 - [Let her be as] the loving hind and pleasant roe; let her breasts satisfy thee at all times; and be thou ravished always with her love.** We thank you right now for making us one and giving us sex to enjoy and express our love towards one another In **Jesus Name Amen!**

FINANCES

Marriage Wisdom Moment

DAY 14

Luke 16:10 Says: He that is faithful in that which is least is faithful also in the much: And he that is unjust in the least is also unjust also in much.

Inspiration: If you are not faithful to God in the little, he asks you to give then you will not be faithful if he asked you to give a lot. Stop telling God when you make a lot of money you will start giving NO! God is looking for you to start giving out of your little, so he can be the one to bless you with a lot. If you will not do it now, you really will not do it later. Give and watch God do great and mighty things. **Be Blessed!**

Practice: Take the time this week to start giving together. Take the time to get your finances in order and begin putting God first. Start giving a little and then increase your giving as God increases your finances until you are giving at least ten percent. Once you are giving ten percent then you will save that same ten percent you give to God until you are living on eighty percent. This is called the 80/20 rule you, live on eighty and you give ten percent and save ten percent. Now just sit back and watch God work to make your finances greater. Do it for a month and try God to see how your finances will grow.

Prayer: Dear Heavenly Father please help my spouse and I give to your kingdom. Help us to trust you with our finances and direct where we are to give to help your kingdom on earth. **Deuteronomy 15:10 says, give generously to him and do so without a grudging heart; then because of this the Lord your God will bless you in all your work and in everything you put your hand**

to. We love you and we did not understand how to give until now. Help us give what you require and Thank you right now for the overflow of blessings because of our giving. Your word says in **Like:6-38 Give, and it will be given to you. A good measure, pressed down, shaken together, and running over, will be poured into your lap. For with the measure you use, it will be measured to you.** Thank you Lord in **Jesus Name Amen!**

DATE NIGHT

Marriage Wisdom Moments

MOVIE NIGHT

Movie Night how about going to the store and buying a movie bucket to make popcorn in and pick up each other's favorite candy or food for the movie night. How about getting a bottle of wine and choose something to watch you both enjoy? Put the kids to bed early and enjoy each, others company with laughter. If the night leads to sex, then just enjoy it. Date night is the quality time you need to spend with each other.

Date Night Simplified:

1.Movie Night pick a movie you both enjoy.

2. Pick up popcorn bucket and favorite candy and food.

3. Pick up a favorite drink or bottle of wine.

4. Put kids to bed early if you have them.

5.Sex is not a must but if you want to then why Not!

6.Enjoy some quality time laughing and having fun together.

COMMUNICATION

Marriage Wisdom Moments

DAY 15

Genesis 2:7 And the Lord God formed man of the dust of the ground and breathe into his nostrils the breath of life, and man became a living soul.

Inspiration: God created us in his image and therefore our first relationship should be with him. If a man or woman do not have a relationship with God how do you expect for them to have one with you! Your Marriage should be a reflection of our relationship with our heavenly father! **Be Blessed!**

Practice: If you never had a relationship with Christ then the first thing you need to do is ask God into your heart and ask him to be your Lord and Savior. Put God first in your life by going into some prayer time in your private place. Make sure it is a place where you can lock the door and talk to God about all that is on your heart. Then ask God what you can do for him. Do it every day and that is how you will build a loving relationship with God. It is the same as spending quality time with your spouse.

Prayer: Dear Heavenly Father, help me to know you better and help me to establish a loving relationship with you like I have with my spouse **Mathew 6:6 says, "But when you pray, go into your room and shut the door and pray to your Father who is in secret. And your Father who sees in secret will reward you."**

Your word also says in **Psalm 91 that He that dwelleth in the secret place of the Most High Shall abide under the shadow of the Almighty will say of Jehovah, He is my refuge and my fortress; My God, in whom I trust.** Thank your Lord that this payer is answered in **Jesus Name Amen!**

LOVE

Marriage Wisdom Moments

DAY 16

Proverbs 4:23 Says: Above all else guard your heart for everything you do flows from it.

Inspiration: when you absolutely love someone, it will flow from your heart. You will show your love by what you do and not just by what you say. Love is a heart issue not just a talk issue! **Be Blessed!**

Practice: Take this week to show your spouse you love them by what you do instead of just saying it by routine. Do something different like bring dinner home on your way from work or stop and get flowers or if finances are tight stop and pick a flower off a tree or go to the library and pick out his or her favorite novel or movie. There are so many things you can do different from your heart.

Prayer: Dear Heavenly Father, teach me how to really show love to my spouse from my heart and not do things out of routine. **1 Peter 4:8: says, above all, love each other deeply, because love covers over a multitude of sins.** Help me to get out of this box I have put myself in and see things differently. Your word also says in **Proverbs 3:3-4: Let love and faithfulness never leave you; bind them around your neck, write them on the tablet of your heart. Then you will win favor and a good name in the sight of God and man.** Thank You this prayer is answered in **Jesus Name Amen!**

TRUST

Marriage Wisdom Moments

DAY 17

Proverbs 11:13 Says, A gossip betrays a confidence, but a trustworthy person keeps a secret.

Inspiration: Let us be trustworthy in our marriages. Husbands and wives let us not take something we discussed amongst ourselves and then one of you go and tell what you discussed. As a married couple what you both entrusted in each other should remain between the two of you. One of you should not be discussing what you discussed in secret. **Be Blessed!**

Practice: Take this week to learn to keep your private matters and conversation amongst you and your spouse private. Learn not to tell everyone everything that is happening in your life and your marriage, some information should be kept sacred. The bible tells you not to let the left know what the right is doing.

Prayer: Dear Heavenly Father help me to keep my marital business between you, me, and my spouse. **Proverbs 26:17 says, He that passeth by, and meddleth with strife belonging not to him, is like one that taketh a dog by the ears.** Help me to know what not to talk about with others unless you have appointed them to speak to us about an issue. Help me to see that when we talk to others about our marital business that is not qualified that they may not have our best interest at heart. Thank You Father that this is done! in **Jesus Name Amen!**

RESPECT

Marriage Wisdom Moments

DAY 18

1Peter 2:17 Says, show proper respect to everyone, love the family of believers, fear God honor the emperor.

Inspiration: Respect is due to everyone and love your brother's and sister's in Christ. When we respect each other, we honor God? Let us honor God by being respectful to our spouses. I find it funny that we will respect our boss at work and our pastor but, will not respect our own spouse. Respect is the most important thing we should be doing in our marriages. Do not let the enemy get you in a position of disrespect! That is one of the first things the enemy tries to do before he leads you to an affair and a divorce. Keep the respect level strong in your marriage and you will win every time. **Be Blessed!**

Practice: Take this week to learn how to respect your spouse. If you yell to communicate then start talking more calmly If you're looking at your spouse in a negative way because of something you know then block that thing and forgive your spouse and start showing them you respect them regardless.

Prayer: Dear Heavenly Father help me to learn how to respect my spouse no matter what I know and what I see. **Titus 2:7 says, show yourself in all respects to be a model of good works, and in your teaching show integrity, dignity.** Help me to realize when I have respected others over my spouse and let me correct that behavior. **Philippians 2:3 says, Do nothing from rivalry or conceit, but in humility count others more significant than yourselves.** Thank, you Lord that this prayer is answered in **Jesus Name Amen!**

DISAGREEMENTS
Marriage Wisdom Moments

DAY 19

Proverbs: 25:2 Says, He that hath no rule over his own spirit is like a city that is broken down without walls.

Inspiration: You are in control of the way you treat your spouse, God is watching how you control your spirit in different situations that occur in your marriage. Stop blaming your bad attitude on your spouse and get in control of yourself and decide to keep a good and contrite spirit. **Be Blessed!**

Practice: Take this week to practice self-control, that means start paying attention to how you react to certain things that may occur this week. If you fly off the handle at anything you deem negative this week then apologize and next time decide to have a better reaction to a situation. Start watching yourself and change what you see.

Prayer: Dear Heavenly Father help me to control my own spirit. Help me control my own reactions to situations I deem negative. **Philippians 4:7 says, And the peace of God, which surpasses all comprehension, will guard your hearts and your minds in Christ Jesus.** I understand that you give me that control and so with that being said I cannot say any more that my spouse made me do it. **Proverbs 3:5-6 says, Trust in the Lord with all your heart and do not lean on your own understanding. In all your ways acknowledge Him, And He will make your paths straight.** Thank you, Lord, for all your help in this matter in **Jesus Name Amen!**

SEX

Marriage Wisdom Moments

DAY 20

Proverbs 6:32 Says, but whoever commits adultery with a woman lacks heart and understanding, he who does it is destroying his own life.

Inspiration: Adultery is a choice, not something that just happens, so if you are making this choice you are stupid. The bible says you destroy your own life and family when you do it. Remember adultery is premeditated so no excuses. Adultery occurs in the head long before it occurs in the bed so, if you are thinking of doing it Stop Now! REPENT!!!! And turn from it. Ask God to keep you from sin and he will. **Be Blessed!**

Practice: If you have been playing around with the idea of adultery you better think twice #1 God is watching and he knows your thoughts and your next move. #2 God does not like it when you have an affair because you are not cheating on just your spouse you are also cheating on God. Remember God said What God put together let no man separate.

Prayer: Dear Heavenly Father I need your help; I have been playing around with the idea of an affair and I am sorry. I repent for thinking this way and I ask you right now to deliver me from separating the marriage you have blessed me with. **Hebrews 13:4 says, Marriage is to be held in honor among all, and the marriage bed is to be undefiled; for fornicators and adulterers God will judge.** I REPENT right now for thinking and planning an affair and please forgive me. Thank you for all your help I believe and receive that I am delivered from adultery and the thought of adultery in **Jesus Name Amen!**

FINANCES
Marriage Wisdom Moments

DAY 21

Proverbs 13:11 Says, wealth obtained by fraud dwindles, but the one who gathers by labor increases it.

Inspiration: Money gotten by robbing or cheating someone will be lost fast, but the one who works honestly for the money it will last. We as married couples should not be defrauding anyone. Don't you know God is watching what you are doing to get money? When we cheat someone out money you are cheating God because the earth is the Lords and the fullness of it. Let us make money God's way and let him make you rich **Be Blessed!**

Practice: Take today to stop cheating in your finances. First you need to stop cheating God by **tithing** and then begin to **pay yourself** the same tenth you give God then **save** a tenth and lastly you need to **live** on the rest of what you have and you **will begin** to see the **blessings of God** pour out in your life so you don't have to cheat anyone.

Prayer: Dear Heavenly Father help me to do business honestly in your sight **Philippians 4:19 says, and my God will supply every need of yours according to his riches in glory in Christ Jesus.** Thank you for helping me to understand I do not have to do business in an under handed way because your word also says, **Luke 6:38 Give, and it will be given to you. Good measure, pressed down, shaken together, running over, will be put into your lap. For with the measure you use it will be measured back to you."** Thank you, Lord, that this prayer is answered in **Jesus Name Amen!**

DATE NIGHT
Marriage Wisdom Moments

Let us Go out!

How about dinner and a comedy show or how about a picnic in the park for lunch or maybe a stroll in the park or near the ocean? How about a place you use to enjoy when you first started dating? Just pick something to do that you both enjoy and that is cost effective. God needs for you to have a date night so that your marriage can last and so you can spend some quality time with each other.

Date Night Simplified

1. Do something you both enjoy.

2. Make it fun

3. Make it cost effective

4. Quality time is the goal

5. The marriage needs a date night to

rekindle any fire that may have died in your marriage.

COMMUNICATION

Marriage Wisdom Moments

DAY 22

Proverbs 10:11 Says, the mouth of the righteous man is a well of life, but the mouth of the wicked conceals violence

Inspiration: When you marry a man or woman of God things, they speak will be life to their spouse, but if the spouse you marry do not know God they will speak from a worldly mindset. Are the words your spouse speaks a well of life? or a well of violence and negativity? Are you married to someone who encourages you? or are you married to someone who provokes you to anger and negativity? If you are married to a spouse that speaks life to you then you are blessed, but if you have a spouse that speaks negatively to you then you need to pray for their deliverance. **Be Blessed!**

Practice: If you are a spouse that speaks negative then take the time this week to get to know God and his word via the bible or a preacher you respect. Begin to see what God says about you and begin to speak what God speaks. **Psalm 139:14 says. Thank you for making me so wonderfully complex! Your workmanship is marvelous how well I know it.** Sometimes we hang around the wrong influences and we begin to speak what they are speaking, let us line up with the word of God and begin to say what God says.

Prayer: Dear Heavenly Father, help me to get saved and learn your word, will and way. Allow me to know what you have to say about my spouse and I and allow me to speak what you speak about us. Forgive me for not knowing and speaking your word over our lives.**1 John 1:7 says, But if we walk in the light, as he is in the light, we have fellowship with one another, and the blood of Jesus his Son cleanses us from all sin.** Lord I desire to be a positive speaking well over my life and over my spouse's life. Help me to live the life you designed for my spouse and I to live. Thank you that this prayer is answered In **Jesus Name Amen!**

LOVE

Marriage Wisdom Moments

DAY 23

Proverbs 3:3-4 Says: Let love and faithfulness never leave you; bind them around your neck write them on the tablet of your heart. Then you will win favor and a good name in the sight of God and men.

Inspiration: Always keep the love in your marriage and remember why you married your spouse. Never lose sight of the love God has blessed you with. Yes, it may seem that the grass is greener on the other side, but you do not see the brown grass at the root. Let Love lead you both into the happiest marriage you ever had. Allow God to be the head of your love and you will always be in love with one another. **Be Blessed!**

Practice: This week let us start showing each other love every day by putting God first in your marriage and prayer. As you pray together let God show you what each other desires and do them. Let God take your marriage from glory to glory using you both.

Prayer: Dear Heavenly Father Thank you for the love you have blessed me with in my marriage. Your word says in **Ecclesiastes 4:12 says, a threefold cord is not easily broken** and I ask you to be that third cord. **1 Corinthians 16:14 says, let all that ye do be done in love.** Lord we thank you that every day with you as the head of my marriage our love will continue to grow and grow. In **Jesus Name Amen!**

TRUST

Marriage Wisdom Moments

DAY 24

Proverbs 16:3 Says, commit to the Lord whatever you do, and he will establish your plans.

Inspiration: When you make a commitment to trust God, he will make our plans come to pass. When we trust one another, whatever plans we make will be done. God wants us to have a strong commitment with each other to the point that when we pray on anything together, he will make those plans come to pass. We should never break trust with one another when we are married because it causes all kinds of problems and insecurities. God wants us to love honor and trust one another. **Be Blessed!**

Practice: Take this week to make sure there are no secrets in your marriage make sure you both have told each other everything especially if it is something recent you have not shared. If the secret is old and way back when but it has a potential of causing major problems, then just tell God and Repent!! Of it and do not look back. Make sure you keep trust in your marriage from here on out and make trust your main commitment.

Prayer: Dear Heavenly Father help me to be trusting in my marriage. Help me to live my life according to your word, will and way. Help me to continue to share everything good or bad with my spouse so I will not leave room for the enemy to enter in. **Zechariah 8:16-17 says, These are the things that you shall do: Speak the truth to one another; render in your gates judgments that are true and make for peace; do not devise evil in your hearts against one another, and love no false oath, for all these things I hate, declares the Lord."** I thank you for helping me to be trustworthy. In **Jesus Name Amen!!**

RESPECT

Marriage Wisdom Moments

DAY 25

James 3:9 -10 Says, with it we bless our lord and Father and with it we curse men who have been made in the likeness of God. From the same mouth come both blessings and cursing. My brethren these things ought not to be.

Inspiration: As a married couple we have times when we curse one another and bless one another, but that should not be that way if we absolutely loved and respect each other. God does not want us to live every day being disrespectful to our spouses, everybody deserves respect no matter how or who they are. Respect is also earned and not just given so If you want respect then you also must earn it. **Be Blessed!**

Practice: Take this week to see the respect level in your marriage. Is it high or is it low?

If it is low, then work on being more respectful in how you do or say things and get that respect level on high. If you speak with disrespect, then change that immediately it is not always about the other person. If you are reading this right now this is about you making changes. God will always work on the one who believes their spouse need to be changed the most.

Prayer: Dear Heavenly Father please help me to respect my spouse on a high level. Help me not to speak in a disrespectful way or tone. Your word says as I respect my spouse, they will show me love. **Titus 2:7 says, show yourself in all respects to be a model of good works, and in your teaching show integrity, dignity.** Thank you for all your help in this matter In **Jesus Name Amen!**

DISAGREEMENTS
Marriage Wisdom Moments

DAY 26

1Peter 5: 8-9 Says be alert and of sober mind. Your enemy the devil prowls around like a roaring lion looking for someone to devour. Resist him standing firm in the faith because you know that the family of believers throughout the world is undergoing the same kind of sufferings. Be Blessed!

Inspiration: The uncommon spouse anticipates and resist anyone attempting to inject doubt, fear, or strife into her home environment. When you are a wife, mother, husband, or father you will guard and protect your family and home with all cost. You will not allow anyone to bring foolishness to your home so that it will cause friction with your spouse and children. Know, recognize, and see when trouble is trying to come in your home. Check your friends and family and remember the enemy can only get in when you invite him in. **Be Blessed!**

Practice: Take the time this week to check yourself to see if you are carrying foolishness into your home by way of friends, family, gossip or work related problems that you may take home to discuss with your spouse that may cause stress and argument. Once you recognize it is you bringing in the foolishness then stop and rebuke Satan for using you in a negative way in your own home. Ask God forgiveness and do not allow him in again.

Prayer: Dear Heavenly Father help me to see when the devil is using me to bring foolishness into my home to cause a negative atmosphere. **Ephesians 4:31-5:2 says, let all bitterness and wrath and anger and clamor and slander be put away from you, along with all malice. Be kind to one**

another, tenderhearted, forgiving one another, as God in Christ forgave you. Therefore, be imitators of God, as beloved children. And walk in love, as Christ loved us and gave himself up for us, a fragrant offering and sacrifice to God. Forgive me Lord and allow me to be a positive force in my home instead of a negative one. I thank you for my deliverance now in **Jesus Name I pray Amen.**

Sex
Marriage Wisdom Moments

DAY 27

1 Corinthians 7:1-40 Says, Now concerning the matters about which you wrote: "It is good for a man not to have sexual relations with a woman." But because of the temptation to sexual immorality, each man should have his own wife and each woman her own husband. The husband should give to his wife her conjugal rights, and likewise the wife to her husband. For the wife does not have authority over her own body, but the husband does. Likewise, the husband does not have authority over his own body, but the wife does. Do not deprive one another, except perhaps by agreement for a limited time, that you may devote yourselves to prayer; but then come together again, so that Satan may not tempt you because of your lack of self-control. ..

Inspiration: The bible tells you right there that sex is for married couples so we should be enjoying it to the fullest. God designed sex for the married couple for not only to bring in Godly offspring but for us to become one and to keep the devil from having us go out and have sinful sex. The bible clearly lets each person know that we are to have sex with one another, and we are not to keep sex from each other. If you keep sex from one another the consequence is that Satan will tempt you to be with someone else. Let us start enjoying more sex. **Be Blessed!**

Practice: If you're not having sex the way God intended for you to have it, then let's take this week to find the time and maybe buy something sexy or just put something on sexy and surprise your spouse, Once you set the tone let them know how much you love them and how much you love making love to them. Sometimes our spouse needs to hear they are satisfying you in the bedroom. Let them know they are sexy and beautiful/handsome in other words just let your spouse know how you feel. Let love have its way in your heart and let your guard down and just enjoy the moment.

Prayer: Dear Heavenly Father thank you for the gift of sex and thank you for creating marriage so we can have satisfying holy sex. Thank you that even when I do not feel sexy you have given me a spouse that thinks I am sexy. **1 Corinthians 7:5 says, Defraud ye not one the other, except [it be] with consent for a time, that ye may give yourselves to fasting and prayer; and come together again, that Satan tempt you not for your incontinency.** Thank you for our love and work in me to feel sexy and give me the desire for love making with my spouse. Your word says above we are not to deprive one another. Thank you for a **LONG-LASTING SATISFYING SEXUAL LIFE WITH MY SPOUSE** in **Jesus Name Amen!!!**

FINANCES

Marriage Wisdom Moments

DAY 28

Proverbs 19:14& 31:11 Says, houses and wealth are inherited from parents, but a prudent wife is from the Lord. Her husband has full confidence in her and lacks nothing of value.

Inspiration: The uncommon spouse has money talks together with their family routinely. Our homes should be running like a business meaning we should NOT! be running out of anything. We should be budgeting knowing what is coming in and what is going out. Our spouses should know what is going on financially. We as wives should make sure there is nothing our family needs or wants. **Be Blessed!**

Practice: Take this month to practice making

and following a budget and then began to take inventory of the things needed in the home and began to buy in bulk especially if you have small children. When you buy things in bulk like toilet paper, soap, personals etc. It cuts down on times in the month you would have to go buy them, also if you buy six months' worth of stuff you would only have to go to the store twice in a year you, see it saves time and money. In my home I buy stuff three months at a time and that works for us. Do what works for you. Practice the eighty twenty rule where you give to charity ten percent and then you save that same ten percent and then you live on the eighty percent that way you are giving and saving and paying your bills.

Prayer: Dear Heavenly Father help me to be a prudent spouse help me to be more responsible with the finances you have trusted me with. **Proverbs 27:12 says, A sensible man watches for problems ahead and prepares to meet them. The simpleton**

never looks and suffers the consequences.
Help me Heavenly Father to get a budget and
begin giving and saving as your word says in
**Luke 6:38 Give, and it will be given to you.
Good measure, pressed down, shaken
together, running over, will be put into
your lap. For with the measure you use it
will be measured back to you."** Help me to
understand that a budget is a map to financial
freedom so I know what I can always do in
my finances. Help me run my home like a
business so my family has no need. Thank
you for your help and I know this prayer is
answered in **Jesus Name Amen!**

DATE NIGHT
Marriage Wisdom Moments

SEXY SPA NIGHT

Giving each other massages is a great way to spend a romantic night in together. Set the mood with scented candles, soft music and low lighting and take turns working out the kinks and making each other feel great. If you are going to try this option for a low-cost, romantic date night, it is worth putting in the effort to really create a relaxing atmosphere. This means cleaning the house, getting rid of clutter (spas are known for their minimalist decor, after all) and brightening up the space with fresh cut flowers and other nature-inspired accents. Just make this date night fun and sexy.

Date Night Simplified

1. Spa Night

2. Clean up

3. Set the tone and atmosphere

4. Give each other massages

5. Be sexy and have fun.

COMMUNICATION

Marriage Wisdom Moments

DAY 29

Galatians 5:22 Says, But the fruit of the spirit is love, joy, peace, forbearance, kindness, goodness, faithfulness, gentleness, and self-control.

Inspiration: Do you know that marriage teaches us the fruits of the spirit? love, joy, peace, forbearance, kindness, goodness, faithfulness, gentleness, and self-control and without these we cannot be like God? That is why we should never give up on our spouses. They help us to be more like our heavenly father. The process of marriage is not always peachy but, God promises us the victory and blessing in the end. Do not let little things spoil your marriage, stay focused and let God lead. A marriage built on the rock (Jesus Christ) will always be successful no matter what! **Be Blessed!**

Practice: If you are the one who likes to give up every time things do not seem to go right then take this time to see what God maybe trying to change in you in your marriage. Maybe God is trying to change your controlling ways which would be self-control on the spiritual fruit list or maybe God is teaching you how to keep the peace in your marriage. Whatever it is it's developing that fruit in your life so stop giving up and start asking God what he is teaching you in your current situation.

Prayer: Dear Heavenly Father, please help me not to give up on my marriage and my spouse every time there is bad communication between us. Your word says in **Matthew 19:6: So, they are no longer two, but one flesh. Therefore, what God has joined together let no one separate."** This means that marriage comes from you, and therefore I should not end my marriage.

Help me to understand that just because we had a communication breakdown does not mean I should be thinking about ending my marriage. Thank you for teaching me the fruit of the spirit through my spouse therefore making me to be more like you. **Galatians 5:22-23 says: But the fruit of the Spirit is love, joy, peace, forbearance, kindness, goodness, faithfulness, gentleness, and self-control. Against such things there is no law.** Thank you for longevity in my marriage and for teaching me not to give up so easily. I thank you for my deliverance in this matter in **Jesus Name Amen!**

LOVE

Marriage Wisdom Moments

DAY 30

Song of Solomon 4: 1-6 Says, behold thou art fair my love, behold thou art, thou hast doves' eyes within thy locks, thy hair is as a flock of goats that appear from mount Gilead. Thy teeth are like a flock of sheep that are even, shorn which came up from the washing where of everyone bear twins and none is barren among them. Thy lips are like a thread of scarlet and thy speech is comely: thy temples are like a piece of a pomegranate within thy locks. Thy neck is like the tower of David builded for an armory, whereon there hang a thousand bucklers, all shields of mighty men. Thy two breasts are like two young roes that are twins, which feed among the lilies. Until the daybreak and the shadows flee away, I will get me to the mountain of myrrh and to the hill of frankincense.

Inspiration: The uncommon spouse keeps a mental love journal of their spouse. Solomon was not only letting his wife know how much he loved her, but he was telling her how sexy she was in his rendition of how she looked to him. He had his heart, eyes, and feelings on the love he has for her. When we keep that mental journal of love our hearts will always be in love with our spouse. In this scripture he loved everything about her, he loved her all the way down to her toes and that is how it supposed to be. We should always love everything about our spouse and be grateful for them. **Be Blessed!**

Practice: Take this week to study your spouse and make mental notes of the things they say, they like or love and let us begin to do those things. Show that love and appreciation for the spouse God has given you. Give your spouse all your attention this week and complement them on their looks and on things they do for you. Let your spouse know they mean the world to you.

Prayer: Dear Heavenly Father help me to love my spouse and make a mental diary of him/her just like Solomon did for his wife. **1 John 3:18 says, Dear children, let us not love with words or speech but with actions and in truth.** Help me to complement my spouse more and help me to express my love and appreciation for them. **Ephesians 5:25 says, Husbands, love your wives, as Christ loved the church and gave himself up for her,** Thank, you for helping me Love my spouse the way you would have me too. Thanks again Lord, for your help in this matter in **Jesus Name Amen!**

TRUST

Marriage Wisdom Moments

DAY 31

Proverbs 12:4 & 31:11 Says, a virtuous woman is a crown to her husband, but she that maketh ashamed is as rottenness in his bones. The heart of her husband doth safely trust in her, so that he shall have no need of spoil.

Inspiration: The uncommon spouse can be trusted by those they love. Be that spouse that hold what your spouse desires dear. Be that spouse that can be trusted in everything if its finances let us be honest if its other relationships let us be honest. Let us be that spouse that no matter what! you can be trusted. Remember God is watching, and he knows what you have been doing so be aware. Trust is a powerful thing and should never be broken. When we have trust in our marriages it helps us to focus on the most important things in life and it helps us get things accomplished. Trust is always knowing what my spouse says is the truth. **Be Blessed!**

Practice: Let us take this day to do whatever you promised you would do and then continue to do the next thing you said and the next. You should desire to be trustworthy in your marriage so from this day forward you will speak the truth and be truthful. Remember what we sow that we will also reap so be a spouse who can be trusted.

Prayer: Dear Heavenly Father help me to be a spouse who can be trusted. As your word says what you sow that you shall also reap is so true and all I want to reap is the truth. **Proverbs 3:5-6 says, Trust in the LORD with all your heart and lean not on your own understanding; in all your ways submit to him, and he will make your paths straight.** Help me live the truth, tell the truth and be the truth so help me God. I thank you now father for my deliverance in this area in **Jesus Name Amen!**

LORETTA A. PITTMAN

Prayer of Salvation

Dear heavenly father I come to you on behalf of(Insert Name) confessing that you are Jesus the son of God and that I believe in my heart that you died on the cross for my sins. I confess that I desire to be saved and get to know you better. I confess that I did not know you before now and now I seek a real relationship with you. I know I am saved, and I will be set free from the strongholds in my life as I walk along with you and build a real and strong relationship with you. Thank you, Jesus, that now I am saved and free to build a real strong relationship with you in **Jesus Name Amen!**

Marriage Prayer

Dear, Heavenly Father we come to you as husband and wife asking you to save our marriage. Lord we believe your word when you say in **Ephesians:22-28, Wives, submit yourselves unto your own husbands, as unto the Lord. For the husband is the head of the wife, even as Christ is the head of the church: and he is the savior of the body. Therefore, as the church is subject unto Christ, so let the wives be to their own husbands in everything. Husbands love your wives, even as Christ also loved the church, and gave himself for it.**

That he might sanctify and cleanse it with the washing of water by the word, That he might present it to himself a glorious church, not having spot, or wrinkle, or any such thing; but that it should be holy and without blemish. So, ought men to love their wives as their own bodies. He that loveth his wife loveth himself. Thank you, Lord, that your word is true and will not come back void as we walk in your statues and obey your commandments. Thank you, Lord, that we already believe that you sent Jesus to die for our sins and because we believe in Jesus we are saved. Thank you, Lord, for saving our marriage and giving us new eyes for each other through the predestination you already designed just for us. We love you and we consider our marriage saved in **Jesus Name! Amen.**

About the Author

Loretta A Pittman is a woman of God, wife, mother, educator, marriage and relationship counselor, and author. I have a master's degree in Christian Counseling and a Bachelors in Christian Education. I have been married for thirty-two years to my hansom husband William K. Pittman and I have four grown children and four grandchildren.

I have been a believer since 1995. I am the author of A Cup of Daily Wisdom for Your Marriage. I own several online businesses and I am the administrator of the Marriage Café a face book community where we do a weekly ministry called Marriage Café.

References

Source: https://bible.knowing-jesus.com/topics/Submission

All Scripture was found In the King James Bible and NIV Bible

https://athealth.com/topics/test-your-own-marriage-satisfaction-2/

https://www.biblehub.com/1_kings/14-9.htm Berean Study Bible

If you would like prayer for your marriage just leave your request at www.dailymarriagewisdom.com or inbox us and like us on Face Book at www.facebook.com/marriagecafe1. You can also follow us on Instagram at https://www.instagram.com/marriagecafe1/

Make sure to subscribe to our You Tube

Channel at
https://www.youtube.com/user/MarriageCaF
e1/videos?view_as=subscriber

We also podcast on
https://marriagecafe.podbean.com
and Spotify and Apple Podcast

Notes

Notes

Notes

Notes

GO AND GET YOUR COPY NOW!!!!!!